Expectancy

A Caregiver's Story of Navigating Family
Issues Between Retirement and Transition

Marvin D. Bryson

Uzma—

Your practice has helped me in ways that I couldn't imagine. I hope this book helps you or someone you love. I'm presently working on a 2nd edition with new chapters on skilled nursing, hospice and palliative care. You've inspired a new chapter on self-care.

With gratitude!

MR

ISBN: 1537703536
ISBN 13: 9781537703534

For my daughter Lakaiha who
reminds me every day what life is truly about.

ACKNOWLEDGEMENTS

Throughout my life's journey, I have been fortunate to have had many mentors, both academic and professional. The lessons they imparted to me, along with those from the streets are at the basis of my personal doctrine of always trying something new when presented with the opportunity.

I first became aware of book publishing when my childhood friend, Stephen Jackson undertook creating a scholarship guide in his early twenties. I found another source of inspiration in a kindred spirit/scribe, Dru Vincent Hunt who authored a fictitious piece on an American expatriate's exploits in Europe, as well as my friend Joseph B. George who published a memoir on his experiences in the first Gulf War.

While admiring their courage to endeavor into authorship, I never dreamed that one day I myself would have something worthwhile to say. So to Steve, Dru, and Joe, my sincere thanks for showing me the way.

My creative partners in this endeavor are Mr. Ken Watts of MECHKW Design, and Mr. Thomas Scott, Jr. of La Scène Media Group. Ken's expertise helped me realize a cover design that I can be proud of, and Thomas' editing of my words took what I hope to convey to a level I could not have reached on my own. I appreciate you gents more than you know.

Lastly, to my family both Love and Bryson, and extended family; you are why I am who I am. One love.

PREFACE

July 25, 2016 was the day I sold our family home. I was 53 years old at the time and had been my ninety-year old mother's primary caregiver for just over four years. Like many children with a parent that realizes an extended life expectancy, I didn't plan to be a caregiver, but kind of settled into the position by default.

As I sat in a coffee shop waiting for the call to pick up my mom's settlement check, I felt that familiar twinge of shock, sadness and melancholy that has overcome me many times in the past few years. The home sale was simply the latest of many steps, jolts, and necessary evils I've had to grabble with on my caregiving journey.

Having experienced the death of my father 16 years earlier and being tasked by him to settle his estate, I had come to appreciate what he was able to establish as a legacy for his wife and family. We both thought he was well-prepared, however, I've come to realize just how woefully unknowing we were regarding issues that arise for individuals who live ten, twenty and thirty years or more into retirement.

With this book, I hope to shed some light on this shadowy subject that many of us don't address as it is unpleasant to think about, much less walk through. I'm not an attorney, insurance agent, or other individual attempting to sell you something, but rather an ordinary guy with an unremarkable education, sharing his experiences in hopes of making someone else's walk a little more informed in the event they have to deal with what I've been through.

TABLE OF CONTENTS

Chapter 1

My Introduction the World of Estate Administration

My introduction to the world of estate administration came in the mid-nineteen-nineties at the ripe young age of thirty-four. I remember it like it was yesterday because its genesis came in the form of a rare phone call from my father requesting my presence.

Dad was old school - a child of the Great Depression, military veteran of Korea and Vietnam, and the literal personification of the strong silent type. So if he reached out, you knew it was serious business. Some of my clearest memories of him involve life lessons, particularly in regards to finance. As an elementary-aged boy, he would call me into his room, throw a pile of cash on the bed, and task me out to count it. While doing so, he often lamented on the value of real estate, more importantly being wise enough to maintain generational wealth, or property handed down from parents to their children. His pet peeve was parents that were smart enough to attain property but didn't train their children on how to keep it.

Later as a teen and young adult, I would come to understand his quasi-obsession through the many stories of how his mother's family had managed to acquire over 100 acres of land at the turn of the century. Over the course of three generations, family ownership had dwindled down to just 25 acres, 15 of which he ultimately carved out into three five-acre plots for himself and his sisters. His efforts in doing so literally took more than a decade of shifting through bureaucratic red-tape and extended family communication issues.

I learned so much from my dad, not from what he said, but more so by observing who he was and what he did. I feel fortunate to have been raised by such an intelligent, hard-working, honest guy. As I write these pages, it's dawned on me that his work to maintain his family's legacy came about much in the way mine has - out of necessity.

So back to the aforementioned phone call. When I arrived at my parent's house, my mom pointed me upstairs to my parents' bedroom, and much like his cash counting lessons of my youth, my dad asked me to sit down at the foot of the bed and proceeded to lecture me on his estate plan. His instructions were verbal, simple, and clear enough to follow. Much to my surprise, my dad had decided to forego a will, and he then proceeded to explain to me why in discussing the rules and laws of administering an intestate estate both on the Federal/IRS level and for the state in which he resided.

For those of you who may not know, intestate is a legal term for a person who has died without having made a will. While this strategy was planned out and worked for my Dad in his particular situation, I strongly advise one to seek out legal counsel when developing an estate plan.

My Dad's lecture came a few months after he retired, and a full two years before he passed away. Upon his death, I proceeded as instructed in settling his estate, and his legacy has provided for my mom and his children, grandchildren, and unmet great grandchildren for nearly 17 years.

In year 12, my mom's health took a drastic turn for the worse, beginning my journey into discovering just how much more is required in navigating family issues between retirement and one's final transition.

My dad, Charles Bryson, Jr., Korea, 1950s

Chapter 2

The Accidental Caregiver

Like many around the world, I was directly affected by the 2007-2008 Global Financial Crisis. Some partners and I launched a business in 2004 on the west coast. Our venture required raising large sums of money for media projects we were developing. We were adequately capitalized administratively, but couldn't sustain any production work largely due to lending institutions tightening their belts by not lending to companies with thin track records. So in short, we couldn't fund any product to sell and eventually dissolved the business.

Faced with the possibility of going back to work as an employee or continuing down the entrepreneurial path, I decided on neither. I had just enough savings left to take nine months off in order to recharge and plot my next course of action. The only question was where?

Around this same time, my aging mom was starting to show telltale signs of mental decline to the point where she needed help with the day-to-day activities like cleaning, driving to the doctors, grocery shopping, etc. In addition, the old neighborhood was on the down-turn, so my siblings and I decided - or rather I concurred with their decision to move her closer to my sister a few states away.

It was a no-brainer given that: 1.) with the relative real estate values, the move would result in a financial boon and 2.) an improved quality of life for her as she would be just around the corner from my sister, and eventually one of my two brothers who had also purchased a home nearby.

While discussing where I should land with my sister, she casually mentioned that she could use some help with mom.   My brother also offered up his house as a place to stay until he and his wife were ready to relocate. So joining my mom and sister seemed like the move to make.

It had been nearly seven years since I lived near my family. In the time I was away, my mom had knee replacement surgery and began to display early signs of dementia. On the occasions I returned home, I didn't really notice her decline simply because my visits literally lasted two or three days. Yet after my first few months back with her, I came to realization that she needed much more assistance than I ever imagined.

In the Preface, I spoke of "jolts" and "necessary evils." The first jolt I experienced was realizing that I had to take on the role of parenting my parent. With her increasing age and frailty, my mom's behavior became noticeably passive aggressive, as she would even display juvenile histrionics whenever she needed help. I would also observe her struggling with budgets and bill paying and offered to take over managing her finances - an offer in which she enthusiastically accepted. The first necessary evil was cajoling her into recognizing that if she continued to drive, she presented a great danger to herself and others. Surprisingly enough, she gave up her keys rather easily.

To facilitate our mother's daily life, my sister and I agreed to split certain duties. I took over grocery shopping, pharmacy runs, etc., while she handled doctor's visits, social activities like church, and other things women do together like going to the beauty shop or nail parlor. Becoming your parent's parent is an extremely difficult role to digest emotionally, but simple in retrospect when compared with what lie ahead.

As we settled into deeper into our routine, I took a menial swing shift job as my savings were running out. I also came to realize that wages in a mid-sized Southern town of two-hundred-fifty-thousand people are not close to on par with those in major cities, particularly with my skillset. So my "regroup plan" was turning out not to be a plan at all.

Eventually my brother and his wife moved into their new house, and I found myself not leaving the area after a year, but moving into my mom's house with her as I was already doing her shopping, paying her bills, and maintaining the place.

Just after I moved in, my mother began to have health episodes that required frequent emergency room visits. After one drawn out ER visit, her dementia spiked noticeably, resulting in a pronounced memory loss. She would begin to repeat things not once, but over and over as her memory was deteriorating. Shortly thereafter, my oldest brother passed away suddenly of a heart attack, further exacerbating her mental condition as she struggled to deal with the loss of her first born.

Given my experience with handling my Dad's estate, my family looked to me to settle my brother's affairs, which took another year and a half. So without warning, my six-month to one-year regroup sojourn had morphed into two and a half years.

Moving forward, things were more or less stable for the next year personally (professionally was another story altogether, but I'll touch on that later), until my mom had another health episode that required her being hospitalized for eight days. At that moment, we all realized how woefully unprepared we were for the events that were unfolding.

Since I had been the family member to deal with legal and estate issues, I slipped right into my role, not realizing there would be no turning back in my role as caregiver.

Mom, sister and me, Ashville, NC airport, 2002

Chapter 3

I've Got the Power

The purpose of this book is to empower readers to navigate family issues in caring for a loved one between retirement and transition.

Essentially, my journey was one of reaction, not pro action. This chapter is about my first pro or reactive steps in getting our family's situation on track, and could be a practical first step for anyone. In any event, my first proactive step was obtaining a General Durable Power of Attorney as it's known in my mom's home state, or a Durable Power of Attorney generally under the law.

A Power of Attorney (POA) can be the most important of all legal documents, for it allows one to open and close bank accounts; buy and sell cars, homes or other real property; open, close, or make changes to utility accounts; etc., as an Attorney-in-Fact for the designee (or my mother in our case). I use the word can, because I am also my mother's Federal Fiduciary and Trustee (for a trust instrument), both of which do not recognize a Power of Attorney as I was to later discover. But that fact is immaterial regarding the POA and how it's the generally accepted document that allows one to act on matters the designee or principal can no longer handle him or herself.

As discussed in Chapter 2, becoming your parent's parent is extremely difficult to digest emotionally and practically. For me, the biggest hurdle was actually acknowledging it. Once I took ownership of the situation, I was able to take steps towards remedying things. My big brother literally told me that I had to think of our mom as if she were my child in a sense, because in her condition, she wasn't really able to understand what was in her best interest anymore. At first I was taken aback by his statement, but then came to realize it was based on years of him being her caregiver at a time when she was still highly functioning.

Prior to my mom's first hospitalization, she and I had agreed that I would take over managing her budget and finances. Because of our mother-son dynamic trust was established, it was simply a matter of me acting as a combination of a file-clerk and bookkeeper on her behalf, basically reviewing her incoming correspondence, evaluating it to determine how it might affect her financially, and then managing her accounts payable and receivable.

I would simply have her sign when and where required regarding property taxes, checks, etc., and we got along well this way for a time. Her hospitalization and subsequent thirty-day stay in a rehabilitation center, however, changed everything for us from a personal and legal standpoint.

Jobwise, the Family Medical Leave Act of 1993 (FMLA) was a blessing to me. FMLA is a United

States federal law requiring covered employers to provide employees job-protected and unpaid leave for qualified medical and family reasons. Reasons include: personal or family illness, military leave, pregnancy, adoption, foster care, and other issues that may arise. The act allows eligible employees to take up to twelve weeks of unpaid leave during any twelve-month period to attend to the serious health condition of the employee, or their parent, spouse, or child.

Since we were basically in crisis-management mode, I did a little research and created my own POA on the fly, and filed for FMLA on my job.   In my mom's home county, POA's are recorded at the Register of Deeds office and require a specific amount of witnessing and notarization before being recorded for a fee.

I highly recommend one consult an attorney regarding any legal documents. My creation of our initial POA was sufficient temporarily, but not nearly as complete, accurate, and thorough as the subsequent POA our attorney drew up. Suffice it to say that we use the attorney's version of the POA now, not mine.

Regarding FMLA, my mom's primary physician actually charged a fee to complete her paperwork. In addition, the company I was working for at the time required that I use any and all vacation leave I had up to eighty hours, and then any remaining FMLA leave requested would be allocated as unpaid leave for up to twelve weeks within a fiscal year, or one year from approval, e.g., February 24, 2014 through February 24, 2015.

FMLA is highly complex and subject to interpretation by employers. One's employer's human resources department should have their policy on hand and assist you in navigating their process, while also providing the necessary forms for the patient's primary physician to complete. Once your FMLA is approved, I strongly recommend that you A.) completely understand your company's polices and rules for requesting time off under FMLA, and B.) that you keep a record or log of communication of requests for time off to your employer, and a log of time actually taken off.

Filing for FMLA at work to cover yourself, and obtaining a valid POA legally to handle your loved one's day-to-day transactions that he or she could do for him or herself, but are no longer able to, proved to a practical and pragmatic first steps for me. Lastly, your FMLA paperwork must be renewed or refiled annually.

Your situation may be different. So again, I strongly recommend one seek legal counsel when creating any aspect of an estate plan.

In subsequent chapters I'll provide a list of documents you may want to consider, and a Glossary of terms that I learned along the way to help you better communicate with attorneys, physicians, employers, and agencies you may encounter on your journey.

Chapter 4

A Man Without A Plan Is Lost

As I sat to reflect on our family's situation, I had more questions than answers. I've always lived by the motto that: "an educated man may not know everything, but he knows where to find it". So my research began.

As with any financial situation with which I find myself confronted, my first step was reaching out to my accountant. She is a CPA and Enrolled Agent with the Internal Revenue Service (IRS), so I am confident that she stays abreast of the latest and greatest changes with the US tax code, and always offers sound tax advice. She suggested I come back to her regarding tax strategies once I had developed a comprehensive plan with an attorney who specialized in Elder Law.   My accountant's advice had saved me countless hours and monies regarding my mom's present tax strategy and I will be forever grateful to her.

Taking her advice, I approached several law firms in our area and found that like other legal specialties, Elder Law has its own niche. Whereas the more recognized legal specialties like personal injury and worker's compensation offer a free initial consultation, the elder lawyers I contacted each charged anywhere from $350 to $700 for an initial consultation.   Most offered to roll up or include the consultation fee into the services provided if one proceeded in estate planning with them.

I've had the good fortune to work for some pretty savvy entrepreneurs in my professional life that taught me to recognize that the most expensive service may not be the best option. Similarly, the least expensive service may not be the worst option. One has to discern who they feel will provide the best service notwithstanding pricing, so I settled on a firm which I felt confident could deliver.

My initial consultation went swimmingly. The attorney I choose was well prepared and asked all the questions I had anticipated as informed by my research. He also had a few questions I had not anticipated, but could answer as I had literally compiled a file that contained all my parents' vital information from healthcare, to pension income, to real property, and banking. My father's status as a Veteran offered even more options for my mom that I was completely unaware of, but informed of by our attorney.

The following is a list of legal documents we settled on as the pieces of our estate plan based on my family's particular needs:

- Last Will
- Durable Power of Attorney
- Health Care Power of Attorney
- Advanced Directive Regarding a Natural Death
- Authorization for Release of Protected Health Information

- Asset Protection Trust
- Personal Care/Caregiver Agreement

It's a rather comprehensive list and all the items may not apply to your situation.

Over the next few months, I worked with our attorney on my mom's estate plan. Many of the aforementioned items were taken care of right away, while others which fell under the purview of a federal, state or local agency, and/or a private entity that would have to be dealt with separately

Upon completion of our estate plan, I organized what I like to call a "signing meeting" for my mother, brother, sister, and me to execute the documents drawn up by our attorney. I made every effort to educate my family before the meeting. Moreover, I strongly advised them to write down any questions, comments, or concerns they had so they could be addressed by our attorney at the meeting.

Thankfully, I have a family that is built on strong bonds of trust and cohesion. I think it comes from the fact that my parents were from strong, intact families, and that my father was a career Airman having served just over twenty-two years in the Air Force. As you may know, families serve right along with their fighting man or woman and sacrifice greatly with long separations and moving about the country and the world for that matter. I'm quite confident that my mom's grit, and our military lifestyle is the discriminating factors in while our bond is so strong.

Bryson family photo, 1962

Chapter 5

Family Members as Caregivers

Our mom's latest hospitalization was my first experience in having to deal with a substantial health crisis. Both our father and brother had died suddenly, so it was more a matter of sorting out the aftermath, and not an ongoing circumstance. As most of us know, doctors treat symptoms in hopes that they can determine their cause. In my mom's case, this took a few days, and she ultimately ended up in the hospital for eight days in total.

The illness that had led to her hospitalization was responsible for yet another spike in her dementia and reduced level of cognitive functioning. So upon her release from the hospital, she was immediately admitted to a rehabilitation center. Needless to say, my sister, brother, and I were truly taken aback at this point.

Navigating a rehab situation is haphazard at best. At the outset arise the usual immediate questions such as: How long is the stay? What's it going to cost? Unfortunately for us, there were no immediate answers.

The first week of rehab consisted of being evaluated, assigned a care team, and settling in. During this entire time, our care team who were very professional and proactive, measured my mother's situation and then schedule a meeting with us. We even had a billing specialist who sorted out her insurance coverages and explained them to us.

Ultimately she ended up spending a month in rehab, mostly to help her regain her strength and mobility, and assess the level of care that would be required upon her release. In the interim, I took the time to resolve my FMLA application at work, and begin the elder law firm search I spoke about earlier.

HIPPA restrictions are a nightmare for family members as it restricts access to one's medical records. So if you are a person's child, you literally do not have access to your mom or dad's medical records under the law.

HIPPA is the acronym for the Health Insurance Portability and Accountability Act that was enacted by Congress in 1996. Protection and Confidential Handling of Health Information is a key piece of the act and requires health care providers and organizations, as well as their business associates to follow certain procedures that ensure the confidentiality and security of Protected Health Information (PHI) when it is shared, handled, received, or transferred. These restrictions include family members' access to records. So obtaining an Authorization for Release of Protected Health Information will become a high priority for you as a caregiver.

About two weeks before my mom's scheduled release from the rehabilitation facility, we had a meeting with her care team. They stated that in order to determine the true level of care she would ultimately require, she would "need someone around". Naturally, I would only grasp the true meaning of her "needing someone around" after the first several weeks following her return home.

In brief, her release included a certain number of visits from a nurse practitioner, physical therapist and occupational therapist to administer care and assess her recovery. So I literally needed to be "around" to manage and facilitate that entire process, along with her taking care of basic household needs i.e. cooking, cleaning and medication management. FMLA was truly a Godsend for those first two months as it allowed me to be there for my mom and our family.

At the end of the first month, it became clear that a caregiver would be required during my work hours as my mom could no longer cook her own meals or manage her medicine. Thus my time out of the house was literally limited to work, shopping, and the occasional hour of personal time since I didn't feel comfortable with my mom being alone for more than an hour or two at maximum.

The hiring of a caregiver would put a strain on my mom's budget, but was doable in the short term. Fortunately, our attorney brought to our awareness a Veteran's Administration program for widows that we were able to take advantage of to help cover the additional caregiver expense. Moreover, my sister's schedule allowed her to take on the task.

There are many tax and legal machinations involved when hiring a caregiver, not to mention the practical implications with managing schedules, discipline, and payment. At the end of the day, our attorney had drawn up a formal caregiver agreement, that stipulated caregiving would be done under the auspices of a contractor or 1099 arrangement in lieu of a W2 or employee relationship. Employee situations involve the implications of various state, federal, and other tax withholdings that we simply could not afford.

I highly recommend consulting both a tax professional and a legal professional prior to entering into any such engagement. Moreover, I suggest a thorough discussion of the arrangement with your family member. Our situation revealed that communication and understanding could be issues, particularly regarding the tax implications of the contractor that received 1099 income in that the caregiver contractor is responsible or liable to pay any and all taxes and withholdings derived from that income.

Suffice it to say that my sister and I working together to care for our mom was and is a labor of love. And although we entered into the process with the best of intentions, it truly became a challenge for both us schedule-wise, and me in particular because I shared my mom's home with her. Over the years, we reached out to community organizations both public and private for guidance, assistance, and counseling.

I was pleasantly surprised by the plethora of options available. And although securing assistance isn't easy, it's very possible.

Mom, College Graduation
Morristown (Tennessee) Teacher's College, 1947

Chapter 6

Outliving Your Savings

The subject of this chapter, particularly outliving one's savings is the biggest challenge a family faces when a loved one realizes an extended life expectancy.

As discussed in Chapter 1, my father felt confident that the pension, savings, and investments he had accumulated would see he and my mom through their retirement years. In our family's case, so far so good, but the selling of our family home was more a necessity than a choice as I'll discuss later. For now, I think it prudent that I go back to caregiving for a moment.

Over the next couple of years, my sister and I settled into our caregiver routine for our mom with me "being around" evenings and weekends since I was living in the same household; and with her coming by from roughly 10 a.m. until 2 p.m. to make sure that she got her breakfast and took her medications on time.

My work hours were from six a.m. until two-thirty p.m., so it worked out to where mom wasn't alone for more than an hour or two at most.

While my sister and I shared responsibility for caregiving during the week, she had other obligations that made her unavailable most weekends, with the exception of a few hours after church on Sundays. So I was on the hook literally seven days a week. This situation was exacerbated when my brother's plan to relocate to the area never came to fruition. Just as he and his wife were getting settled, they received an offer they literally couldn't refuse, inducing them to make an unforeseen move to another state.

So while their support was much needed and greatly appreciated, their change of plans would leave the onus of the caregiving on me. And before I knew it, a year had passed where I literally took just a handful of time off from daily caregiver responsibilities. Honestly, going to work felt like a break as it was emotionally less stressful.

During that same time, I began the process of completing the paperwork for the Veteran's Widow Pension our attorney advised me of. There were several major discoveries along the way, the first being that the Veteran's Administration does not recognize a duly executed Durable Power of Attorney, and if a third party would be administering pension funds, they would be required to qualify as a Federal Fiduciary.

Becoming a Federal Fiduciary is a tedious process akin to qualifying for a mortgage or obtaining a Federal Security Clearance, complete with criminal background investigations, credit checks, and the whole nine yards. It's so cumbersome in fact that there are literally companies out there that will act as your agent to complete the process for a fee. In addition, you're dealing with the government, so it literally takes months to complete - in my case, seven. Fortunately for us, the county we live in has a Veterans' Service Office where I was able to secure first-rate assistance.

As most homeowners well know, household maintenance items and other small unexpected expenses can stealthily nibble away at one's savings. It took note of this when Mom's luxury car which was falling into disrepair was costing more to maintain than it was worth. In her state, an annual vehicle inspection is required, and after a particularly high repair estimate to keep the car on the road - for the third year in a row I may add, we decided to essentially junk it.

So after thirteen years, I sounded the alarm with my brother and sister that we needed to look at ways to tighten up mom's budget because she was headed in the direction of outliving her savings.

And, after nearly two years of seven-day-a-week caregiving duty, coupled with the feeling of guilt that I was neglecting my adult-daughter and grandchild; I was literally nearing my breaking point. So it became time to explore other options.

Chapter 7

<u>Generational Wealth and Medicaid</u>

Generational wealth or the passing down of assets from one generation to the other is an undiscussed topic for many families. I've read studies indicating that anywhere from fifty to seventy percent of a family's wealth is gone by the third generation.

Unfortunately, this statistic strikes a very personal chord with me as I've also witnessed one side of my family literally squander everything. From my perspective, it was essentially due to miscommunication, a lack of foresight by elders, and the natural discord that can occur in large families. Conversely, the other side, a much smaller family unit, took measures to maintain as much of their hard earned assets as possible - a tradition I am currently fighting to maintain.

While researching in-home care scenarios upon my mother's release, I discovered that the vast majority of programs required patients to be Medicaid eligible. I found this to be true for many assisted living and long-term care facilities as well.

In my mom's state, the income requirement for Medicaid is just under one thousand dollars a month for an individual and fourteen hundred dollars a month for a couple. There is also a resource cap of no more than two thousand dollars. Resources are defined as cash, bank accounts, retirement accounts, stocks and bonds, life insurance, and other investments.

For example, if your retirement income is more than one thousand dollars a month individually, or fourteen hundred dollars a month as a couple, and you have more than two thousand dollars in resources, one basically has to examine the Medicaid Spend Down requirements to determine their Medicaid eligibility.

Many people receive a monthly pension or other retirement income that is too much for them to qualify for Medicaid. Children under 21 years of age, the disabled or blind, and other groups have Medicaid interests too, but my focus in this book is exclusively on retirees.

So retirees with excess income may qualify for Medicaid if they spend the excess income on medical bills. This is what is characterizes the spend down in a nutshell -- medical expenses. As you can imagine, there is a plethora of rules and requirements for each state, so I'm just covering the essence of the Medicaid Spend Down concept here.

I highly recommend that you examine the rules for your state with a qualified state representative. In addition, many states have Ombudsman programs that advocate for elderly patients and can help with navigating long term care issues and concerns for your loved one.

Unfortunately, some people consider the prepaying of funeral expenses or asset transfers to individuals or trust instruments as part of the Medicaid Spend Down. However, the latter is subject to the Medicaid Look Back Period for Asset Transfers and not part of any spend down scenario. On the other hand, prepaying funeral expenses can be a cost-effective way to meet Medicaid's eligibility requirements, especially when considering that funeral costs can range anywhere from ten to twenty thousand dollars. In my mom's state, the funds that are placed into an annuity that is fully backed by the state board of funeral services. I highly recommend that you look into the rules, regulations, and guarantees in your state before entering into any pre-payment agreement.

Regarding trusts instruments, they're extremely complicated, so I won't even attempt to explain them here. However, I do highly recommend you engage an elder law attorney to discuss your options. Although our family currently has had one created, I am in no position to attest to how effective it is, until we have to use it. As I write this, we are thirty-seven months into the sixty month or five-year look back period. So only time will tell, I guess as the law is a living, breathing thing.

Lastly, each state has its own requirements, rules, regulations, and definitions regarding Medicaid eligibility, spend downs, resources, and whether or not to receive or accept Federal Medicaid funds. Moreover, these elements are changing all the time depending on state and national politics. So God speed in navigating your state's system.

Fortunately, we haven't reached the stage where we have to apply for Medicaid to continue my mother's care. I hope and pray that day never comes.

Chapter 8

<u>Assisted Living</u>

In the spring we celebrated my mom's eighty eighth birthday. It was a bittersweet occasion due to her gradual physical decline and continued memory loss.

My comfort level with leaving her alone for a few hours at a time had long since dwindled. There were times when she would attempt to prepare herself some tea or something on the stove and inevitably forget she had left something on, resulting in the burning of a pot or pan and triggering smoke detectors. She would also get up in the middle of the night and turn on the porch light or open the front door in the expectation of a visit from my oldest brother who was now deceased.

Furthermore, she had reached a point that it was better to just agree with her when she thought she was in a different physical location e.g. her parent's or uncle's house; lost the day, date or time; or even didn't recognize us as she often referred to me by my father's or her younger brother's name thinking I was one of them. Earlier on, we thought that our correcting her somehow brought her back, if you will. But as she continued to decline, this effort seemed to upset her more than help. Therefore, we just let her be as it facilitated her being in a relaxed emotional and peaceful mental state.

Almost two years to the date from her last hospitalization, my sister found her on the floor when she came for a regular caregiving session. And while she hadn't broken anything nor appeared to have any serious injuries, the event resulted in a hospital admission of six days. And like before, her transport from the hospital to the rehabilitation center required an ambulance due to her fragile condition.

Having gone through a rehabilitation scenario just twelve months earlier, my sister and I had an idea of what to expect. During our first consultation for this new visit, I got a sinking feeling that mom's condition had deteriorated to the point to where she would require twenty-four-hour care. Ever the optimist and not wanting to upset my sister any further, I kept my concerns to myself while the rehabilitation process played itself out.

The estate planning we had put in place proved useful as we were able to completely manage my mom's affairs, no matter what the scenario this time around. However, we still found ourselves unprepared for the blow we were to receive when it was confirmed that my mom would indeed require twenty-four care upon her discharge. It's truly hard to explain the jolt I felt upon hearing this news. Moreover, we had just a matter of days to make the arrangements. So in spite of my distress, I had to buckle down and move forward.

Thankfully, I had a co-worker who was facing a similar dilemma. She and I served as each other's support system, allowing us to share the latest mishap, struggle or curve ball that came our way as caregivers. I performed my financial due diligence and concluded that my mom's finances dictated that we place her in an assisted living facility in lieu of in home care.

My sister and I started by reviewing a list of local facilities. She had a friend whose mom was in a facility she liked. Yet given it was a two-hour drive each way from where we lived, we both agreed it was off the table. Moving onward, we visited the facility where my co-worker's mom resided. While decent, there was something about the place that just didn't sit well with us. The second place we visited was completely unacceptable. However, we were blessed to find a newly renovated and affordable facility on our third try.

Racked with guilt and emotional confusion, we proceeded with enrolling my mom into an assisted living facility, knowing that it was the only way she could receive the level of care she needed. And although it was literally years in the making, our lives were completely and irrevocably changed within a matter of 72 hours.

Chapter 9

Closing Thoughts

The hours leading up to my mom being transferred from a rehabilitation center into the assisted living facility were a haze of activity, emotion and resolution. Since she was a self-pay client and not on Medicaid, we had to supply her furniture and other essentials. Thankfully, we had the furniture that she needed on hand. We also acted on the advice of bringing along some family photos and an heirloom trinket or two to give her room a feel of familiarity. That suggestion paid off, particularly a photo of the latest edition to our family, my mother's great-grandson as the final piece.

Ironically enough, her first month in the assisted living went better than we imagined. She hit it off with her roommate and had the same homecare routine i.e., visits from a nurse practitioner, physical therapist, and occupational therapist over the course of several weeks. The facility also retained a medical doctor that made weekly calls and serves as some of the resident's primary physician.

Over the coming months, I muddled through work, attempting to figure out what my new normal might be, and wrestling with the emotional shock, sadness and melancholy that came with my situation. I had to, and have to continually remind myself that she's getting the care she needs, and will be taken care of no matter what may happen with my brother, sister, or me. Despite our deepest desires, we simply cannot do what is required for her while having to take care of our own respective families.

What the future holds as well as one's life expectancy remains an unknown proposition despite one's best laid plans. My mom's mother lived to be one hundred and two years old, so with my mom just turning ninety, she actually seems young by comparison.

In laying the plans for her future, it also dawned on me that it had been a full nineteen years since my Dad retired, and sixteen since he passed. So in earnest, I had to take a moment and reflect on the fact that we had managed to do a decent job in keeping my mom comfortable for nearly fifteen years. However, given my grandmother's lifespan, we are literally faced with the proposition of managing my mother's finances in a manner that best serves what could very likely be another fifteen years, or a thirty-year retirement, or more. Needless to say, it's a daunting task, which takes me back to our family home.

In chapter seven, I discussed Medicaid and its rules, generational wealth, trusts, etc. One of the many caveats in the trust instrument we employed is that the property can be lived in and maintained by family, but not rented out in the traditional sense. Therefore, we were faced with attempting to find resources to keep up a property that no one was living in, wanted to live in, and most importantly, that no one could afford to maintain. Ultimately, we opted to convert the property within the trust itself.

Looking to the future, one would think that property, cash and a decent pension might be enough. However, considering that the cost of home care, assisted living and long term care facilities range anywhere from three-thousand to ten-thousand dollars a month, one could easily go through their savings, property, and investments in just a few years.

Therein lies the dilemma, and why I took the time to share my story of navigating my mother's care between her retirement and final transition. Thankfully, she has not transitioned yet, but her illness helped shed a new light on retirement planning that my dad couldn't foresee, and I hadn't considered. And as a result, my actions have been for the most part reactive instead of proactive.

It is my hope that this book will spur readers to take a proactive stance and start a conversation with their loved ones around this issue.

GLOSSARY

1099 Job - A 1099 job is a job that is performed by a self-employed contractor or business owner as opposed to an employee. The general rule is that an individual is an independent contractor if the payer has the right to control or direct only the result of the work and not what will be done and how it will be done. In addition, the earnings of a person who is working as an independent contractor are subject to self-employment tax.

Accountant - An accountant is a person skilled or trained in the maintenance and audit of personal or business accounts and prepares financial and tax reports.

Advanced Directive Regarding a Natural Death - An advance directive regarding a natural death is a legal document which allows one to instruct their primary or attending physician on whether or not they wish to be given life-sustaining treatments and artificially administered nutrition (food) and hydration (water) and to give other medical directions that impact the end of life. Its purpose is to recognize a patient's right to control some aspects of their medical care and treatment, primarily the right to decline medical treatment or direct that it be withdrawn even if death ensues. An advanced directive regarding a natural death is also known as a living will.

Asset Protection Trust - An asset protection trust is a term which covers a wide spectrum of legal structures. Any form of trust which provides for funds to be held on a discretionary basis falls within this category. Such trusts are set up in an attempt to avoid or mitigate the effects of taxation, divorce and bankruptcy on the beneficiary. Such trusts are therefore frequently proscribed or limited in their effects by governments and courts.

Assisted Living - An assisted living residence or assisted living facility is a housing facility for people with disabilities or for adults who cannot or chose not to live independently. The term is popular in the United States but is similar to a retirement home in the sense that these facilities provide a group living environment and typically cater to an elderly population.

Attorney-in-Fact - An attorney-in-fact is someone specifically named by another through a written power of attorney to act for the person and carry out the appointer's personal and business affairs by acting on their behalf, including signing documents.

Authorization for Release of Protected Health Information - Health insurers, employer health plans, medical service providers, and other covered entities - as that term is defined by HIPAA - must obtain a signed authorization from an individual or the individual's legally authorized representative to disclose that individual's protected health information.

Certified Public Account - A certified public accountant (CPA) is an individual who has passed the uniform CPA examination administered by the American Institute of Certified Public Accountants, and who has received state certification to practice accounting. To achieve this designation, an individual usually has to complete 5 years of education, and a certain degree of work experience. Additionally, once an individual becomes a CPA, they typically must complete a certain number of hours of continuing education within specified time periods.

Contractor - An independent contractor is a person, business, or corporation that contracts with an employer to do a particular piece of work or provide goods. This working relationship is a flexible one that benefits both the worker and the employer and is generally done on a freelance basis. The distinction between a contractor and an employee is significant in that employer's pay social security, Medicare, and unemployment taxes for their employees whereas contractors are responsible to pay their own federal social security and Medicare taxes.

Durable Power of Attorney - A durable power of attorney is a legal document that allows a person to act as one's agent, and to continue acting on a person's behalf if that person becomes incapacitated. Individuals planning retirement care for example, will grant a durable power of attorney to someone whom they trust to act as their attorney-in-fact regarding finances, medical treatment, and other important decisions. A non-durable power of attorney is a legal document that generally grants authority on a limited scope to the agent, as opposed to a durable power of attorney that is much more broad in its scope and authority.

Family Medical Leave Act of 1993 (FMLA) – The Family Medical Leave Act of 1993 entitles eligible employees of covered employers to take unpaid, job-protected leave for specified family and medical reasons with the continuation of group health insurance coverage under the same terms and conditions as if the employee had not taken leave. Eligible employees are entitled to twelve workweeks of leave in a 12-month period for:

- The birth of a child and to care for the newborn child within one year of birth
- The placement with the employee of a child for adoption or foster care and to care for the newly placed child within one year of placement
- To care for the employee's spouse, child, or parent who has a serious health condition
- A serious health condition that makes the employee unable to perform the essential functions of his or her job
- Any qualifying exigency arising out of the fact that the employee's spouse, son, daughter, parent is a covered military member on "covered active duty" or

Twenty-six workweeks of leave during a single 12-month period to care for a covered servicemember with a serious injury or illness if the eligible employee is the servicemember's spouse, son, daughter, parent, or next-of-kin (military caregiver leave).

Federal Fiduciary - A federal fiduciary is a person or legal entity authorized by Veteran's Administration (VA) to serve as payee of VA benefits for a beneficiary unable to manage his or her financial affairs. The term federal fiduciary includes the following:

- Spouse-Payee - An incompetent Veteran's spouse who is designated to administer the funds payable for the Veteran and other dependents, if any.
- Legal Custodian - The person or legal entity designated by VA to manage VA funds on behalf of a beneficiary unable to manage his or her financial affairs.
- Superintendent of Indian Reservation - A superintendent or other officer designated by the Secretary of the Interior to receive funds due an Indian beneficiary unable to manage his or her financial affairs.
- Custodian-in-Fact - An emergency, temporary payee for a beneficiary incapable of managing his or her VA benefits, certified by VA when payments cannot be timely made to an existing or successor fiduciary, or when payment to such existing or successor fiduciary would be inappropriate under the circumstances.
- Institutional Award Payee - The chief officer of an institution who is authorized the payment of all or part of the VA benefits due a Veteran who is incapable of managing his or her own financial affairs. The Veteran must be receiving hospital treatment or institutional, nursing, or domiciliary care in the facility. This method of payment is appropriate when VA benefits paid either adequately provide for the needs of the Veteran, or are not substantial enough to require another type of fiduciary.

Elder Law - Elder law is a relatively new specialty in the legal field (early 2000s) devoted to the legal issues of senior citizens including estate planning, health care planning, planning for incapacity or mental incompetence, the receipt of benefits, and employment discrimination.

Enrolled Agent - An enrolled agent is a person who has earned the privilege of representing taxpayers before the Internal Revenue Service by either passing a three-part comprehensive IRS test covering individual and business tax returns, or through experience as a former IRS employee. Enrolled agent status is the highest credential the IRS awards. Individuals who obtain this elite status must adhere to ethical standards and complete 72 hours of continuing education courses every three years.

Enrolled agents, like attorneys and certified public accountants (CPAs), have unlimited practice rights. This means they are unrestricted as to which taxpayers they can represent, what types of tax matters they can handle, and which IRS offices they can represent clients before.

Health Care Power of Attorney - A health care power of attorney is a legal document that allows an individual to empower another with decisions regarding his or her healthcare and medical treatment. A healthcare power of attorney becomes active when a person is unable to make decisions or consciously communicate intentions regarding medical treatments. A health care power of attorney is also sometimes called an advance directive for health care, or a living will.

Health Insurance Portability and Accountability Act of 1996 (HIPPA) - The Health Insurance Portability and Accountability Act of 1996 was enacted to amend the Internal Revenue Code of 1986 to improve portability and continuity of health insurance and health care delivery, to promote the use of medical saving accounts, to improve access to long-term care service and coverage, to simplify the administration of health insurance, and for other purposes. The act's privacy rule regulates the use and disclosure of Protected Health Information (PHI) held by health insurers, employer sponsored health plans, and medical service providers that engage in certain transactions, and includes any part of an individual's medical record.

Hospice – A facility or program designed to provide a caring environment for meeting the emotional and physical needs of the terminally ill. Hospices focus on caring not curing, and in many cases care is provided in the patient's home.

Intestate Estate - A legal term for a person who has died without having made a will.

Last Will - A last will and testament is a legal document that communicates a person's final wishes regarding their possessions. A person's last will and testament specifies what to do with one's possessions whether he or she is leaving them to a person or group or donating them to a charity, and what happens to other things for which he or she is responsible, i.e., custody of dependents.

Living Will - A living will is a legal document that allows a patient to give explicit instructions to be administered when said patient is terminally ill or permanently unconscious. A living will is often referred to as an advanced directive or health care power of attorney.

Long Term Care - Long term is a range of services and supports one may need to meet his or her personal care needs; particularly with respect to retirees and the disabled. Most long term care in not medical, but rather assistance with basic personal care tasks of everyday life. Sometimes referred to as activities of daily living (ADLs) e.g.: bathing, dressing, using the toilet, eating, transferring to or from a bed or chair, managing money, taking medication, and more.

Medicaid - Medicaid is a health care program that assists and low-income families or individuals in paying for long-term medical and custodial care costs that are often required by the disabled and retirees. Medicaid is a joint program, funded primarily by the federal government and run at the state level, where coverage often varies.

Medicaid Look Back - The Medicaid look-back period is the time preceding a person's application for Medicaid during which asset transfers will be scrutinized. A transfer within the look-back period can be questioned and if something of equal value was not received in return by the transferrer, a penalty can be applied that can prevent the transferrer from receiving Medicaid benefits until any imposed penalty period expires. The look-back period is 60 months or 5 years for transfers under the Deficit Reduction Act of 2005.

Medicaid Spend Down - People with low incomes typically automatically qualify for Medicaid. However, people whose incomes exceed the Medicaid income limits, may qualify for Medicaid only if they have medical bills that are equal to or greater than their excess income. The process of subtracting those medical bills for an individual's income is called the Medicaid spend-down.

Ombudsman - An Ombudsman is usually appointed by the government, but with a significant degree of independence, and is charged with representing the interests of the public by investigating and addressing complaints of maladministration or a violation of rights. The typical duties of an ombudsman are to investigate complaints and attempt to resolve them, usually through recommendations or mediation. Some state and local government provide Ombudsmen to provide information and assistance to families in areas including: care planning and family resident councils, resident councils, resident transfer and discharge, and long-term care planning.

Personal Care/Caregiver Agreement - This AGREEMENT is a CONTRACT typically between a family member who agrees to provide CAREGIVER service for a disabled or aging relative, or the PERSON receiving CARE.

The personal care agreement is usually between an adult child and his/her parent, but other relatives may be involved, such as an adult grandchild caring for a grandparent. These agreements formalize the contractor/employee, and employer relationship between the parties and are often required documentation to secure additional retirement or other benefits for the employing party.

Real Property - REAL PROPERTY, also referred to as REAL estate, realty or immovable PROPERTY is any PROPERTY attached directly to land as well as the land itself. It is any subset of land that has been improved through legal human actions. REAL PROPERTIES include buildings, ponds, canals, roads and machinery, among other things.

Self-Employment Tax - Self-employment tax is money that a small business owner or contractor must pay to the federal government to fund Medicare and Social Security. Self-employed persons report their business income or loss on Schedule C of IRS Form 1040 and calculate the self-employment tax on Schedule SE of IRS Form 1040.

Testate Estate - Having a legally valid will. Opposite of intestate.

Trustee - An individual person or member of a board given control or powers of administration of property in trust, generally for the benefit of a third party, with a legal obligation to administer it solely for the purposes specified.

Made in the USA
Columbia, SC
06 October 2018